A MISCELLANY

Compiled by Julia Skinner
With particular reference to the work of Clive Hardy

THE FRANCIS FRITH COLLECTION

www.francisfrith.com

First published in the United Kingdom in 2006 by The Francis Frith Collection®

Hardback edition published in 2006 ISBN 10: 1-84589-328-X ISBN 13: 978-1-84589-328-6

British Library Cataloguing in Publication Data

Did You Know? Derby - A Miscellany
Compiled by Julia Skinner
With particular reference to the work of Clive Hardy

The Francis Frith Collection
Frith's Barn, Teffont,
Salisbury, Wiltshire SP3 5QP
Tel: +44 (0) 1722 716 376
Email: info@francisfrith.co.uk
www.francisfrith.com

Printed and bound in Thailand

Front Cover: **DERBY, THE CORNMARKET 1896** 37779p

The colour-tinting is for illustrative purposes only, and is not intended to be historically accurate

AS WITH ANY HISTORICAL DATABASE, THE FRANCIS FRITH ARCHIVE IS CONSTANTLY BEING CORRECTED AND IMPROVED, AND THE PUBLISHERS WOULD WELCOME INFORMATION ON OMISSIONS OR INACCURACIES

CONTENTS

INTRODUCTION

The power of the Derbyshire rivers - particularly the Derwent - attracted the first real industrialists to the county in the 18th century. Foremost among these were Thomas and John Lombe, who established Derby's silk mill around 1718. Jedediah Strutt's cotton mill at Belper, a few miles from Derby, was founded in 1776, and Strutt also established a calico and tape mill in Derby itself.

The famous Derby porcelain factory was established by William Duesbury in the 1750s and an iron-founding industry followed, helped by local supplies of coal. The building of the Derby Canal by Benjamin Outram in 1796 proved to be a key element in turning a prosperous market town into a leading centre of industry.

Derby's modern growth was due to it being chosen as the headquarters and main workshops for the Midland Railway. Good rail connections soon led to other industries opening for business, and the population rocketed to over 114,000 people by 1901.

One of the major employers in 20th-century Derby was Rolls-Royce, referred to locally as 'the Royce'; cars were made here until 1946, but aero engine production has now taken over; the Derby Museum of History and Industry tells the story of Derby's industrial heritage and features an extensive aero engine gallery, where the locally produced exhibits range from an early Eagle to a modern RB.211 turbofan.

Derby has now become one of the major industrial and engineering centres of the Midlands. Toyota, the giant Japanese car manufacturer, has opened a large new factory on the airfield at Burnaston, and has become a significant employer in the area.

Situated on the edge of the Peak District National Park, Derby is now a vibrant modern city, but still retains much of its Georgian architectural heritage; an idea of what life in Derby was like in its Industrial Revolution heyday can be gained by a visit to Pickford's

House Museum of Georgian Life and Costume, where the rooms are furnished 'in period' - including the servant's bedroom in the attic.

The story of Derby is full of fascinating characters and events, of which this book can only provide a brief glimpse.

THE ROYAL INFIRMARY 1896 37787

DERBYSHIRE DIALECT WORDS AND PHRASES

'Ah've bin up all naight wee a badly rabbit' - I've had a sleepless night.

'Be said' - That's enough, end of conversation.

'Clammed' - very hungry.

'Caded' - spoilt.

'Causey' - pavement.

'Cob' - a bread roll.

'The dogshelf' - the floor

'Mardy' - peevish, childish, easily upset.

'Mizzle' - very light, misty rain.

'Put wood int th' ole!' - Shut the door!

'Scratin' - crying.

'Teggies' - teeth, especially of children.

The phrase ***'a Derby game'*** means a game when two sides from the same town or city play each other, and derives from the Shrovetide football matches between teams from rivalling parishes in Derby.

The famous horse race known as the **Derby** got its name from the 12th Earl of Derby; he was a keen sportsman, and suggested to his friend Sir Charles Bunbury that they should fund a new short and exciting race for young three-year-olds. They decided to run the first race at Epsom Downs in 1780. They tossed a coin to decide which of them would give it a name, and it is by pure chance that the race is not now famous throughout the world as the Bunbury!

HAUNTED DERBY

A ghostly figure in the dress of a Royalist soldier from the Civil War has been reported in the area of the Old Silk Mill pub.

The Noah's Ark pub at the Morledge, on the outskirts of Derby, is said to be haunted by the ghost of Noah Bullock, a 17th-century gentleman counterfeiter who lived on an 'ark' on the River Derwent with his family from where he carried on his illegal occupation. In 1676 he was arrested and appeared before the Recorder for Derby, Sir Simon Degge. Bullock knew Degge well, and in a deal he promised to destroy his ark and give up his counterfeiting activity in return for his life being spared.

There are several ghost stories associated with the cathedral and its grounds:

A ghostly man in what appears to be Jacobite costume has been seen walking into the cathedral, believed by some to be the shade of Bonnie Prince Charlie retracing his steps, as he is said to have attended a service at the cathedral (then All Saints' Church) in 1745.

The area around the cathedral is believed to be haunted by the ghost of John Crosland, a former criminal who became a well-known public executioner in Derbyshire. Crosland originally got into this line of work when he agreed to carry out the sentence of death on his own father and brother in return for a pardon. His ghost is now tormented by guilt and remorse, and wanders the grounds of the cathedral seeking solace.

Also reported around the cathedral are sightings of a White Lady walking down the steps at the rear, a small boy, and a young woman who appears to be weeping.

DERBY MISCELLANY

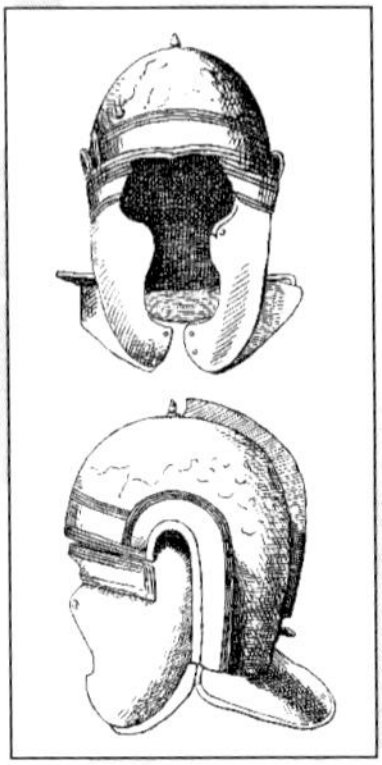

AN ARTIST'S IMPRESSION OF A ROMAN HELMET F6014

The Romans had a fort in the Derby area, known as Derventio (Little Chester); this guarded both a bridge over the Derwent and an important road junction, for it was here that the roads to Chester, Wall, Cirencester, Chesterfield, Buxton and York met. There were a number of small forts strung out along the roads of Cheshire and Derbyshire. These were used to secure lines of communication for the legionary bases at Chester and York, to police the local natives and to regulate the movement of salt and copper ore traffic from Cheshire and lead from the mines of Derbyshire. It might even be possible that Derby had a *mansio*, a relay station for the imperial postal service, where messengers could either get accommodation or a change of horse. How long the fort remained in commission is unknown, but it was still garrisoned in the mid 4th century.

St Mary's Roman Catholic Church in Derby was designed in the Victorian Gothic style by Augustus Pugin (see photograph 37793, opposite). Work began on the £7,000 project in June 1838, and the dedication took place in October 1839. The town's Catholic community had been growing steadily since the Napoleonic Wars, owing to large numbers of Irish immigrants attracted by the prospect of work in local mills.

ST MARY'S CHURCH 1896 37793

ON THE DERWENT 1896 37789

The first Anglian people who colonised the Peak District were known as the Pecsaete, or people of the Peak, while the south of the county fell under the influence of that powerful kingdom of Middle England - Mercia. The Derbyshire area appears to have acted as a buffer between the Anglo-Saxon kingdoms of Mercia and Northumbria for a period, before Mercia finally attained ascendancy by the end of the 8th century. Recent research has suggested that for some time both Anglo-Saxon and Viking people lived in the district of what is now Derby, occupying two areas of land surrounded by water that were known respectively as Northworthy and Deoraby, and were located at the north side of Derby. The name 'Deorby' may derive from an Old Scandinavian word meaning 'the place where deer are seen'.

At the Peace of Wedmore in AD878 between the Danes and the Anglo-Saxon King Alfred, the two sides agreed to split the country into two areas of control (photograph 43677a, left, shows the idealised Victorian statue of King Alfred at Winchester in Hampshire). Deorby (Derby) was absorbed into the Danelaw as one of the Five Boroughs (the others were Stamford, Nottingham, Lincoln and nearby Leicester). The Danes were allowed to settle in the Danelaw, where Danish laws, not Anglo-Saxon, were followed. Each of the Five Boroughs had its own 'army' council at which all freeholding landowners had a right to be heard. Voting was done by a show of weapons, hence the old term 'wapentake' for an administrative area. Each of the Five Boroughs could be expected to field several hundred troops, perhaps more. The townships themselves would have been built in the classic Danish style of narrow timber-framed houses and workshops with thatched roofs and wattle-and-daub walls.

A VICTORIAN STATUE OF KING ALFRED 1901 43677a

This photograph was taken three years after gas lamps had been replaced by electric street lighting. The horse-trams started running in the 1880s and survived until 1904, when they were replaced by electric trams. The electric trams lasted only until 1934, when they too were replaced, this time by trolleybuses.

THE GUILDHALL 1896 37776a

THE ARBORETUM ARCADE 1896 37792

When the Arboretum opened in September 1840 it was the first public park in the country. The land was donated by the industrialist Joseph Strutt, who hired the top landscape designer of the day, John Loudon, to create a park planted with every variety of tree and shrub capable of withstanding the climate. There were three days of celebration to mark the opening, and such was the interest in the Arboretum that the Midland Railway ran special excursion trains to Derby. Photograph 37792, above, was taken in 1896, and shows the main entrance at Arboretum Street. Entrance to the Arboretum was made free in 1882, although visitors were expected to wear their best clothes.

Holy Trinity Church in London Road was originally a private development, and was initially called St George's Church. The developer went bust and the church was eventually sold and renamed.

In the early 10th century, after the Danes of the Danelaw attacked the English kingdoms of the south, King Alfred's son and successor Edward the Elder and his sister Ethelfleda, the 'Lady of the Mercians', went on the offensive; their aim was the complete reconquest of the Danelaw. Derby fell to Ethelfleda's forces in AD918. The fighting at Derby was heavy: the 'Anglo-Saxon Chronicle' tells us that Ethelfleda lost four of her thegns, all killed within the gates of Derby.

IRON GATE 1896 37780x

Built in 1846 at a cost of £9,000 on the site of an earlier church, St Alkmund's Church was named after the son of the deposed Northumbrian King Alured. Alkmund was martyred in AD800 on the orders of King Eardulph, and is said to have eventually been buried in Derby. When St Alkmund's was demolished to make way for the inner ring road, archaeologists had an opportunity to excavate the site for the remains of the old Saxon church. The excavation revealed a basic two-cell church of not later than the 9th century. St Alkmund's might well have been the church of Saxon Northworthy.

In 1756 a factory opened in Derby for the manufacture of porcelain. Thanks to royal patronage it became known by the title of Crown Derby in 1773. The works closed in 1848, but in 1849 William Locke opened a new porcelain factory in King Street. In 1876 the Derby Crown Porcelain Co was floated, eventually opening up in what had been the local workhouse, which was known to the natives as the Bastille. In 1891 the company's name was changed to the Royal Crown Derby Porcelain Co.

In December 1745 Derby was the southernmost point reached by Charles Edward Stuart (Bonny Prince Charlie) during his attempt to reclaim the throne for the House of Stuart from the Hanoverian king, George II. Had Charles not turned back for Scotland at this point, the whole course of British history might have been different. However, supporters for the Jacobean cause did not flock to join the army in the hoped-for numbers: only about 200 had joined at Manchester and Preston, and it used to be thought that only three men joined at Derby, although recent research has turned up a fourth name. Charles was persuaded to return to Scotland and eventual defeat at the Battle of Culloden.

ST ALKMUND'S CHURCH 1896 37785

IRON GATE AND THE CATHEDRAL c1955 D24011

All Saint's Church was granted cathedral status in 1927. Its stately 212ft-high Perpendicular tower still exerts a powerful influence on Derbyshire's biggest city (see photograph D24011, above). The tower was built in the early years of the 16th century, but the rest of the building was completely rebuilt by James Gibbs between 1723-25, during the incumbency of Dr Michael Hutchinson (see page 21).

Derby's cathedral has the oldest ring of 10 bells in the world. The largest bell, the tenor, was cast in 1520, and the youngest bell was cast in 1693. Local tradition says that Bonnie Prince Charlie ordered the bells of the church to be rung when he entered Derby in 1745.

In October 1831 the citizens of Derby rioted, angry at the failure of the Reform Bill on its final vote. Damage was done to houses and business premises of known anti-reformers; the door of the borough gaol was battered in and the prisoners released. In Iron Gate the surgeon Henry Haden attempted to calm things down, but he was pushed to the ground; those who went to his assistance found that he was dead, and the inquest returned a verdict of natural causes. The Reform Act was eventually passed in 1832; this important piece of legislation gave seats in Parliament to the new towns created by the Industrial Revolution, and also extended the franchise. It was a reform that had been strongly resisted by the more reactionary element of British society, and was achieved after over 50 years of agitation from people who felt that those who were creating the wealth of the country should be represented in Parliament.

THE CORNMARKET 1896 37779

Part-way along the steps in photograph D24017 (below) the culvert can be seen where the Markeaton Brook surfaces to join the Derwent. At one time the brook was little better than an open sewer that meandered its way through town; a local name for it was the Shitte Brook. The cells of the old town gaol were situated

below the brook's flood level and some prisoners are known to have drowned during flash floods, whilst others died of 'gaol fever'. In 1932 over £400,000 worth of damage was done in the town centre when a section of the culverting collapsed following heavy rain and the area flooded.

THE MUNICIPAL BUILDINGS AND RIVERSIDE GARDENS c1955 D24017

ALL SAINTS' CHURCH 1896 37783

It is possible that the Derbyshire lead mining industry of the late Middle Ages was operated on some sort of cartel basis. Many smeltors and investors in mines were also merchants; in the 14th century the smelter Thurstan de Boure of Tideswell amassed a fortune operating bole hills and trading in lead at Chesterfield and Derby. A bole hill was in effect a wind-assisted smelter. It was a walled enclosure a few feet in diameter with an opening facing the prevailing wind. It was filled with layers of timber or peat first, then lead ore. This was covered with more timber and then another layer of ore and so on until it was full, then it was topped off with turf. A channel ran from inside the bole to a gathering pool into which the molten lead would trickle. When the wind was in the right direction the bole was fired, and the smelted ore which collected in the gathering pool formed a pig of lead.

Around 1278, Chesterfield merchants were able to grab a larger share of the lucrative market in lead at Derby's expense, thanks to the monks of Dale Abbey who obstructed the navigable Derwent with weirs at Borrowash. Chesterfield was then able to offer an alternative route to London and the Continent via the port of Bawtry on the River Idle.

In 1723 Dr Michael Hutchinson, the incumbent of All Saints' Church, was having trouble with his parishioners. Hutchinson wanted to rebuild the church, which was in a bad state of repair, but the parishioners and the Corporation objected. Not to be outdone, the resourceful Hutchinson acted independently: on the night of 18 February 1723 he had the roof ripped off and the interior demolished. There was little alternative but to rebuild, but Hutchinson had to raise the money himself through public subscription.

LONDON ROAD 1896 37781

Derby was an early player in the tourist industry, thanks to Thomas Cook of Melbourne, a few miles away. Cook's business started out of his work for the temperance movement; his first excursion took the friends of temperance from Leicester to Loughborough and back. Derby was used as the meeting-point for the tourists from the south, south-west, south-east, East Anglia and Lincolnshire who were booked on his Scottish tours. Those needing overnight accommodation were housed at Smithard's Temperance Hotel in the Cornmarket or by Cook himself at Leicester. The following morning the train would depart from Derby, picking up at Chesterfield, Sheffield, Normanton, York, Newcastle and Berwick.

The register of St Werburgh's Church records the marriage of Dr Samuel Johnson, one of England's greatest literary figures, to the widow Elizabeth 'Tetty' Porter in 1735. At the time of the wedding he was 25, and she was 46. When Elizabeth first met Dr Johnson she described him as 'the most sensible man I ever met', and despite the age difference Dr Johnson called the marriage 'a love-match on both sides'. Their wedding is re-enacted in the church every year.

ST WERBURGH'S CHURCH c1955 D24025

A ROLLS-ROYCE 1911 63380

Derby's emergence as a railway centre in the 19th century encouraged businessmen to set up factories in the area, including Qualcast in 1849, Fletchers in 1860, and Leys Casting in 1870. In 1881 the dry-air refrigeration system developed in Derby by Alfred Haslam enabled cargoes of fresh beef and mutton to be brought from Australia, and in 1906 Rolls-Royce opened their factory at Osmaston Road.

In 1895 the Mundy family donated land for Markeaton Park, Derby's second park. (Bass's Recreation Ground had opened in 1867, but it was not laid out as a park.) Osmaston Park opened in 1922, followed by Darley Park in 1929 and Allestree Park in 1948.

The Rolls-Royce Company moved from Osmaston Road to their purpose-built factory in Nightingale Road, Derby, in 1908. One of the famous Rolls-Royce cars made in Derby was the 'Silver Ghost', shown in photograph 63380, opposite, which was considered to be the best production car in the world. In 1946 motorcar production was transferred to Crewe, leaving the Derby branch of the company concentrating all its efforts on designing and building aero engines, work that had started just before the outbreak of the First World War - see page 37.

The centre of Derby was partially redeveloped during the 19th century: both St Peter's Street and Iron Gate were widened, Markeaton Brook was culverted over, the Shambles in the Market Place were demolished, and a new road bridge was built over the Derwent.

IRON GATE AND ALL SAINTS' CHURCH 1896 37780

ST PETER'S CHURCH 1896 37786

THE MUNICIPAL BUILDINGS AND RIVERSIDE GARDENS c1955 D24014

The inhabitants of Derby used to take part in the local Shrovetide football matches, which involved a large number of townspeople although in theory the matches were played between the parishioners of St Peter's and All Saints' Churches. When the pancake bell was rung on Shrove Tuesday the players descended upon the Market Place, where the ball was thrown up and mayhem ensued. As many as 1,000 players could be taking part, rules were few and far between, and the playing area was the streets of the town. It was not unusual for players to finish up with broken arms or legs, and if the ball went into the river or one of the brooks that flowed through the town, the players simply followed. All Saints' goal was a waterwheel at Nuns Mill, which had to be knocked three times for a goal to count. St Peter's goal was a nursery gate about a mile out of town. On Ash Wednesday the game was repeated, but this time restricted to those considered too young to play on Shrove Tuesday. The football matches were disliked by many townsfolk because they caused damage to property and disruption to trade; the mayor William Mousley once tried to put a stop to the custom by using his powers to forbid the bringing of a ball into the Market Place; although he called in the cavalry to assist, his plan was foiled by an old lady called Mother Hope, who hobbled into the Market Place with a ball hidden beneath her skirts before throwing it up for the match to begin. The matches were finally banned in 1860.

The following rhyme describes the churches around Derby, and was traditionally chanted at the beginning of the Shrovetide football match:

Pancakes and fritters
Say All Saints and St Peter's
When will the ball come?
Say the bells of St Alkmun's;
At two they will throw
Says St Werabo
O! very well
Says little St Michael!

THE CENOTAPH c1955 D24012

Inside Derby's cathedral is the tomb of Bess of Hardwick, the Dowager Countess of Shrewsbury. Bess, who died in 1607, was one of the most redoubtable and powerful women of Tudor England. She was said to have a mania for building, and a knack of marrying well to finance it. She was first married at the age of twelve, and as each of her husbands died she became richer. Her fourth, and last, husband was George, Earl of Shrewsbury. He was for many years the custodian of the imprisoned Mary, Queen of Scots; Bess grew tired of this arrangement and left her husband, but even so, when he died in 1590 he left her all his money. Although now elderly, Bess immediately set about the building of Hardwick Hall, a few miles from Derby, which was ready for occupation in 1597. It is notable for the number and size of its windows, giving rise to the saying 'Hardwick Hall, More glass than wall'. It has a huge tower at each corner of the building, topped with decorative open stonework incorporating the letters ES - for Elizabeth Shrewsbury.

England's first silk mills were established in Derby beside the River Derwent; the earliest was sited on an island in the river in 1702 by William Cotchett, and the next was built by George Sorocold c1718 for Thomas and John Lombe. The latter was the first commercially successful textile mill in Britain to use water-powered machinery, and housed machinery used for the process known as 'doubling', or twisting silk into thread. The silk mill became one of the tourist attractions of 18th-century Derby, but some visitors were appalled by the conditions there: one visitor complained of the 'heat, stinks and noise', and another in 1835 was distressed by the unhealthy appearance of the children who worked there. The mill was rebuilt after a fire in 1910, and is now the home of Derby's Museum of Industry and History in Silk Mill Lane, off Full Street, but the fine wrought-iron gates of the original building, made in 1725, can still be seen outside the museum.

One of Derby's famous modern artworks is the 'Boy and Ram' statue, which illustrates an old Derbyshire folksong, 'The Derby Ram', about 'the finest ram that ever was fed on hay'. Rams have become closely associated with Derby; its football team has one as its emblem, resulting in its nickname 'The Rams'. Rams are also incorporated in the city's coat of arms. The statue, by Wilfred Dudeney, used to stand in the Castlefields Main Centre, but was moved in 2005 to the Riverside Gardens, near the Council House, during the construction of the Westfield extension to the Eagle Centre. When construction is completed, the statue will be relocated in a prominent position.

One colourful reminder of Derby's silk industry can be found on the huge mural on the end of the Old Silk Mill pub in Full Street, which was painted in 1986 as part of the Derby Community Arts Project. It depicts the Silk Trades Lock Out of November 1833 to April 1934, when 800 silk workers went on strike. The employers resisted the strike, and then took the view that the oath which the workers had sworn when they combined into an early form of trade union was illegal, and refused to employ any workers who were members of such a union. All silk workers who continued to be members of the union were 'locked out' of the mills until they had renounced their membership. The dispute dragged on for some months before reaching a conclusion best described as a draw for both sides. The event is commemorated annually by a Silk Mill March and Rally organised by the Derby Area Trades Union Council.

ST ALKMUND'S CHURCH
1896 37784

DUFFIELD, KING STREET c1955 D159026

In the 13th century one of the greatest fortresses in England was situated just a few miles to the north of Derby at Duffield. It belonged to Robert de Ferrers, Earl of Derby. In 1263 the earl rebelled against Henry III's authority and was defeated. Though his possessions were ordered to be forfeited to the Crown, the earl was pardoned on condition that if he rebelled again he would lose everything. In 1266, following the defeat of the barons at the Battle of Evesham, Robert took to the field again, assembling a force at Duffield where he was joined by Baldwin de Wake, Lord of Chesterfield. On their way north to meet up with reinforcements from Yorkshire, the rebels were attacked by royal troops and forced to shelter behind the defences at Chesterfield. The earl, who was suffering with gout, had hidden in the parish church behind some sacks of wool left by traders at the Whitsuntide fair; he was betrayed, captured and taken to Windsor in irons. The Ferrers estates were confiscated, and Duffield Castle demolished.

The view shown of Duffield in the 1950s in photograph D1593090, below, is still much the same today. By the side of Tamworth Street is an old stone bridge over the River Ecclesbourne which was made of stone salvaged from the castle ruins. All that remains of Duffield's fortress now are the foundations of the keep.

DUFFIELD, TOWN STREET c1955 D1593090

ST MARY'S BRIDGE c1960 D24055

THE ARBORETUM 1896 37790

VICTORIA STREET 1896 37778

As well as being famous for producing exceptional motorcars, Rolls-Royce are also renowned for producing aircraft engines. This tradition began with a 200hp engine, the Eagle, which was produced at the Derby factory. The company went on to become one of the world's three leading aero engine manufacturers. A half-sized version of the Eagle, the Falcon, was fitted to an aeroplane made by the Bristol Aircraft Company, which proved to one of the most successful machines of the First World War. The Rolls-Royce engines gained widespread recognition as a result of the long-distance flights of the 1920s. In 1927 the Kestrel was selected for use by the RAF, but it was the Merlin that became the most famous of all piston engines, powering the great fighter planes of the Second World War - the Hurricane and the Spitfire - as well as the bombers, such as the Lancaster, the Halifax and the Mosquito. The development of the Whittle jet engine was taken over by Rolls-Royce in 1943, and the switch from piston to jet engines placed the company in the forefront of aero engine development. The RB211 engine, introduced in 1972, became one of the most widely used engines in the world, not only for aircraft, but also for pumps and power turbines. The supersonic plane Concorde was powered by the Olympus 593 Turbojet, developed and powered jointly by Rolls-Royce and the French company SNECMA. Currently, the Rolls-Royce engines for the exciting new Airbus, the A380, are being made in Derby.

Derby Museum and Art Gallery holds work by the Derby-born artist Joseph Wright (1734-97), who was a master of candlelight and firelight scenes.

It is said that in the crusading period a Syrian variety of daffodil was introduced to Duffield, brought back from the Holy Land by a soldier.

By 1840, no less than three railway companies were operating lines to Derby from Nottingham, Leeds and Birmingham respectively. Within five years they had amalgamated to form the Midland Railway and, benefiting from its central position on the east coast line, Derby became a major railway centre and terminus. The Midland Railway established its headquarters and main workshops here, and under Matthew Kirtley the works were transformed. As

ST PETER'S STREET c1955 D24050d

well as continuing with repairs and maintenance, Kirtley oversaw an expansion programme that gave Derby the capacity to construct locomotives. In 1851, goods engine No 147 was rolled out of the erecting shop, the first of over 2,900 new steam locomotives that would be built there. By 1862 the workshops were employing over 2,000 people, and more foundries soon followed in the town to provide other components for the burgeoning railways.

SPORTING DERBY

Derby County legend Steve Bloomer (1874-1938) was one of the early superstars of football. He was widely regarded as the best player of his time. He made his England debut in 1895 and went on to score 28 goals in his 23 games. This remained the England scoring record until 1956. He captained his country whilst a Derby player. In total, he scored 293 goals in 474 League games. His extraordinary life took in everything from commercial product endorsement to four years in a German prison during the First World War. His name is remembered in the first line of the Rams' anthem: 'Steve Bloomer's watching, helping the fight, guiding our heroes in the black and the white'.

The county cricket ground at Derby was at one time located inside a racecourse. Until 1939 both horse racing and cricket took place at the Nottingham Road venue. Horse racing was stopped due to poor attendances and the cricket club took over the whole site. However, the old jockeys' changing rooms were still being used by the cricketers until 1982, when new purpose-built facilities were introduced.

Derby was at the heart of the most successful era in British baseball. The game was introduced to Britain by a Derby man, Francis Ley, in the early 1890s. The game enjoyed good levels of support, often, as in Derby's case, being closely allied to football clubs. Derby were one of the leading teams, winning the English Cup in 1897. Footballer Steve Bloomer was at one time also one of the baseball club's top players.

Derby was the birthplace of successful cyclist Max Sciandri. He was born in the city in 1967 and turned professional in 1989. The mid 1990s saw him at the height of his powers, winning a stage of the Tour de France in 1995, and an Olympic bronze medal in the road race at the Atlanta games in 1996.

THE GUILDHALL 1896 37776

IRON GATE 1896 37780V

QUIZ QUESTIONS

Answers on page 48.

1. What important event for Derby occurred in 1977?

2. Robert Bakewell was a famous craftsman who had a workshop in Oake's Yard, St Peter Street. He died in 1752 and is buried in St Peter's Church. What was his skill, and where in Derby can you see a particularly fine example of his work?

3. Why was it said that silk might have caused the death of John Lombe in 1722?

4. To what was a French prisoner of war referring when he commented: 'If the English call this playing, it would be impossible to say what they call fighting'.

5. By what name is a Derby hat (the American term) known in England?

6. What tragic 'first' in British history was achieved by Charles Rolls, one of the founders of the Rolls-Royce Company?

7. The tower of All Saint's Cathedral is said to be the second highest in England, at 212ft. The tower is open on certain days of the year, when visitors can climb to the top, where fine views of the city can be seen. How many steps do you have to climb to reach the top of the cathedral tower?

8. What was the former role of the building that now houses the Standing Order pub?

9. What was a Derby Rib used for?

10. Which German city is twinned with Derby?

A DERBY POLICEMAN 1896 37790x

RECIPE

DERBYSHIRE FRUIT LOAF

Ingredients
450g/1lb mixed dried fruit
225g/8oz sugar
300ml/½ pint hot (milk-less) tea
1egg
450g/1lb self-raising flour
Half a teaspoonful mixed spice
Half a teaspoonful ground nutmeg
2 tablespoonfuls marmalade

Put the dried fruit, sugar and hot tea in a bowl and leave to soak overnight.

To make the loaf:
Pre-heat the oven to 150 degrees C/300 degrees F/Gas Mark 2. Stir the egg, flour, spices and marmalade into the fruit, sugar and tea. Pour into a greased and lined loaf tin and bake for 1½ - 2 hours until firm to the touch, or until a knife or skewer pushed into the cake comes out clean. When cooled, store in an airtight tin. Serve cut into slices, spread with butter.

ST PETER'S CHURCH c1960 D24062

THE CORNMARKET 1896 37779x

RECIPE

DERBYSHIRE OATCAKES

These oatcakes are similar to pancakes, and are served rolled up and filled with either sweet or savoury fillings. Try them with ham, bacon, mushrooms, grated cheese, egg, and sausage, or for a quick snack wrapped around cheese and warmed in a microwave or under a grill, or eat them whilst still warm from the pan, spread with honey, jam or golden syrup. This recipe makes about four Derbyshire oatcakes, which are smaller and thicker than the Staffordshire variety - increase the quantity of milk and water to 900ml/1½ pints to make a larger quantity of thinner oatcakes.

Ingredients

225g/8oz fine oatmeal
225g/8oz plain flour
1 teaspoonful salt
1 teaspoonful sugar
15g/½oz fresh yeast, or 1½ teaspoonfuls quick-acting dried yeast
600ml/1 pint warm milk and water, mixed half and half

Add the salt to the flour and oatmeal. Dissolve the yeast with a little warm milk and water, add the sugar, then leave it until it becomes frothy. When the yeast mixture is ready, mix the dry ingredients with the yeast and the rest of the warm liquid to make a batter. Cover the mixture with a clean cloth and leave in a warm place for 1 hour.

To cook the oatcakes, use a well-greased griddle or heavy frying pan. Put enough batter on the hot griddle to make an oatcake of your own preferred size; cook, and turn after 2-3 minutes and cook for a further 2-3 minutes - both sides should be golden brown. Serve with the filling of your choice.

QUIZ ANSWERS

1. Derby was awarded city status in 1977, as part of Queen Elizabeth II's silver jubilee celebrations.

2. Robert Bakewell was an exceptionally skilled blacksmith. A wrought iron screen made by him can be seen in Derby's cathedral, where it separates the nave and the chancel; the ironwork is so fine and intricately made that it has been compared to lace.

3. By the middle of the 18th century the framework knitting industry around Derby was specialising in silk hose. In 1702 Thomas Cotchett tried to establish a silk-spinning mill at Derby, but had trouble producing thread of good enough quality. Cotchett's associate, John Lombe, worked for a time in an Italian silk factory and returned in 1717 after stealing designs for silk-throwing machinery. George Sorocold built a five-storey mill for Thomas and John Lombe which used this improved machinery, and by 1732 the Derby silk mill was employing 300 workers; however, John Lombe died in 1722 in mysterious circumstances, and it was said that he was poisoned as a contract killing, courtesy of his former Italian employers.

4. The Shrovetide football match that was played through the streets of Derby before the custom was banned in 1860 (see page 27).

5. The Derby is the American name for what is known in England as the Bowler hat.

6. In 1910, as a crowd of several thousand looked on, Charles Rolls became the first man in Britain to die in a flying accident. His aircraft broke in mid-air and crashed during a display at Southbourne Aerodrome in Hampshire.

7. There are 180 steps to the top of the cathedral tower.

8. The Standing Order pub, which opened in the mid 1990s, was previously a branch of the NatWest Bank.

9. A Derby Rib was an attachment used on a framework knitting machine to produce a knitted rib on hose (stockings, or long socks). The machine was patented (in 1759) and produced by Jedediah Strutt, and revolutionised the hosiery industry. Jedediah Strutt was a successful industrialist who used part of his wealth to donate the land for the Arboretum to the people of Derby.

10. Derby is twinned with Osnabruck.

MARKEATON HALL, THE LAKE c1960 D24057

MARKEATON PARK c1960 A200027

FRANCIS FRITH

PIONEER VICTORIAN PHOTOGRAPHER

Francis Frith, founder of the world-famous photographic archive, was a complex and multi-talented man. A devout Quaker and a highly successful Victorian businessman, he was philosophical by nature and pioneering in outlook. By 1855 he had already established a wholesale grocery business in Liverpool, and sold it for the astonishing sum of £200,000, which is the equivalent today of over £15,000,000. Now in his thirties, and captivated by the new science of photography, Frith set out on a series of pioneering journeys up the Nile and to the Near East.

INTRIGUE AND EXPLORATION

He was the first photographer to venture beyond the sixth cataract of the Nile. Africa was still the mysterious 'Dark Continent', and Stanley and Livingstone's historic meeting was a decade into the future. The conditions for picture taking confound belief. He laboured for hours in his wicker dark-room in the sweltering heat of the desert, while the volatile chemicals fizzed dangerously in their trays. Back in London he exhibited his photographs and was 'rapturously cheered' by members of the Royal Society. His reputation as a photographer was made overnight.

VENTURE OF A LIFE-TIME

By the 1870s the railways had threaded their way across the country, and Bank Holidays and half-day Saturdays had been made obligatory by Act of Parliament. All of a sudden the working man and his family were able to enjoy days out, take holidays, and see a little more of the world.

With typical business acumen, Francis Frith foresaw that these new tourists would enjoy having souvenirs to commemorate their days out. For the next thirty years he travelled the country by train and by pony and trap, producing fine photographs of seaside resorts and beauty spots that were keenly bought by millions of Victorians. These prints were painstakingly pasted into family albums and pored over during the dark nights of winter, rekindling precious memories of summer excursions. Frith's studio was soon supplying retail shops all over the country, and by 1890 F Frith & Co had become the greatest specialist photographic publishing company in the world, with over 2,000 sales outlets, and pioneered the picture postcard.

FRANCIS FRITH'S LEGACY

Francis Frith had died in 1898 at his villa in Cannes, his great project still growing. By 1970 the archive he created contained over a third of a million pictures showing 7,000 British towns and villages.

Frith's legacy to us today is of immense significance and value, for the magnificent archive of evocative photographs he created provides a unique record of change in the cities, towns and villages throughout Britain over a century and more. Frith and his fellow studio photographers revisited locations many times down the years to update their views, compiling for us an enthralling and colourful pageant of British life and character.

We are fortunate that Frith was dedicated to recording the minutiae of everyday life. For it is this sheer wealth of visual data, the painstaking chronicle of changes in dress, transport, street layouts, buildings, housing and landscape that captivates us so much today, offering us a powerful link with the past and with the lives of our ancestors.

Computers have now made it possible for Frith's many thousands of images to be accessed almost instantly. The archive offers every one of us an opportunity to examine the places where we and our families have lived and worked down the years. Its images, depicting our shared past, are now bringing pleasure and enlightenment to millions around the world a century and more after his death.

For further information visit: www.francisfrith.com

INTERIOR DECORATION

Frith's photographs can be seen framed and as giant wall murals in thousands of pubs, restaurants, hotels, banks, retail stores and other public buildings throughout Britain. These provide interesting and attractive décor, generating strong local interest and acting as a powerful reminder of gentler days in our increasingly busy and frenetic world.

FRITH PRODUCTS

All Frith photographs are available as prints and posters in a variety of different sizes and styles. In the UK we also offer a range of other gift and stationery products illustrated with Frith photographs, although many of these are not available for delivery outside the UK – see our web site for more information on the products available for delivery in your country.

THE INTERNET

Over 100,000 photographs of Britain can be viewed and purchased on the Frith web site. The web site also includes memories and reminiscences contributed by our customers, who have personal knowledge of localities and of the people and properties depicted in Frith photographs. If you wish to learn more about a specific town or village you may find these reminiscences fascinating to browse. Why not add your own comments if you think they would be of interest to others? See **www.francisfrith.com**

PLEASE HELP US BRING FRITH'S PHOTOGRAPHS TO LIFE

Our authors do their best to recount the history of the places they write about. They give insights into how particular towns and villages developed, they describe the architecture of streets and buildings, and they discuss the lives of famous people who lived there. But however knowledgeable our authors are, the story they tell is necessarily incomplete.

Frith's photographs are so much more than plain historical documents. They are living proofs of the flow of human life down the generations. They show real people at real moments in history; and each of those people is the son or daughter of someone, the brother or sister, aunt or uncle, grandfather or grandmother of someone else. All of them lived, worked and played in the streets depicted in Frith's photographs.

We would be grateful if you would give us your insights into the places shown in our photographs: the streets and buildings, the shops, businesses and industries. Post your memories of life in those streets on the Frith website: what it was like growing up there, who ran the local shop and what shopping was like years ago; if your workplace is shown tell us about your working day and what the building is used for now. Read other visitors' memories and reconnect with your shared local history and heritage. With your help more and more Frith photographs can be brought to life, and vital memories preserved for posterity, and for the benefit of historians in the future.

Wherever possible, we will try to include some of your comments in future editions of our books. Moreover, if you spot errors in dates, titles or other facts, please let us know, because our archive records are not always completely accurate- they rely on 140 years of human endeavour and hand-compiled records. You can email us using the contact form on the website.

Thank you!

For further information, trade, or author enquiries please contact us at the address below:

The Francis Frith Collection, Frith's Barn, Teffont, Salisbury, Wiltshire, England SP3 5QP.

Tel: +44 (0)1722 716 376 Fax: +44 (0)1722 716 881

e-mail: sales@francisfrith.co.uk **www.francisfrith.com**